MIMIKA COONEY

Mindset Make Over

How to renew your Mind and Walk in God's Authority

Mindset Make-Over: How to Renew your Mind and Walk in God's Authority. First Edition.

ISBN 978-1-7322848-5-2

Cover Design (back and front): Mimika Cooney

Editor: Angela McClain

Unless otherwise indicated, all Scripture quotations are taken from the Holy Bible, New International Version®, NIV®. Copyright ©1973, 1978, 1984, 2011 by Biblica, Inc.™. The "NIV" and "New International Version" are trademarks registered in the United States Patent and Trademark Office by Biblica, Inc.™

Please note that Mimika Cooney has made the stylistic choice to capitalize certain words and pronouns that refer to the Father, Son, Holy Spirit, Christ, although it may differ from the stylistic choices of other publishers. For spelling purposes the use of British English is used throughout.

This book and all other materials is published by Mimika Cooney. If you would like more information on Mimika Cooney and her ministry, or would like to purchase more materials, please visit www.MimikaCooney.com

First edition

ISBN: 978-1-7322848-4-5

Editing by Angela McClain

This book was professionally typeset on Reedsy.
Find out more at reedsy.com

Contents

Invitation

As a thank you for purchasing this book I would love to gift you with the digital version of the accompanying Study Guide. Print out this extra tool to help you work through the book as you follow along.

Go to www.mimikacooney.com/mindset to download your free gift.

MINDSET MAKE-OVER

How to Renew your Mind & Walk in God's Authority

#MINDSETMAKEOVER

GET FREE BOOK BONUSES

WWW.MIMIKACOONEY.COM/MINDSET

1

Are you Stuck?

"*I am just stuck... I feel undervalued by everyone around me, making me doubt myself even when I'm doing great... I have no idea how to move past fear and anxiety... it's suffocating! Nothing has worked to give me relief from this pain. Fear grips my heart every night.*

These are some of the heartbreaking comments I received in a survey when I asked *"What is your single biggest challenge with your mindset?"* If you can relate to any of these answers, I'm sure it is the reason you are here reading this book right now.

What is going on here? There is a battle raging in our minds. We are constantly at war. As Children of God, we are saved by grace, but it doesn't mean that the battle stops raging. We are perpetually in a battle to take our thoughts captive. Why? Because our stinking thinking has debilitated us. We need to look underneath the hood to figure out how we can renew our mind with the tools God has given us. And we need to do that *over and over again*.

This book is designed for you if you're constantly feeling worried, afraid, anxious, doubtful, angry, depressed, or confused. You know God is calling you to greatness, but you feel far from great. Your relationships are a hot mess and the daily drama drains you. You feel out of control, but you crave peace. You are sick and tired of being sick and tired. You are stuck thinking of the worst-case scenario for everything (someone say drama queen!). You feel far from God, yet you crave intimacy with Him.

If you said *yes* to any of the above, let me tell you darling, you are not alone. The war in your head is what happens with all believers. It starts the moment we get saved. We think life will automatically become perfect and pop out a microwave bag of blessings as soon as we accept Jesus as our personal Savior. Unfortunately, that is not how it works. We have to *do* the work to see God's promises manifest in our lives.

What I'm going to share with you is a journey that I have been through personally, the lessons that I have learned through the life of hard knocks and my struggles. Learning from others' experiences is wise if we can avoid the same mistakes. After you hear from me, you are going to learn how to get unstuck from that stinking thinking. You may not realize it, but your thinking habits might be holding you back. We are going to cover how to move past self-doubt and feeling worthless and how to activate the power of God's Word, so you can walk in victory for the rest of your life, no matter what your circumstances are.

I'm sure you would find realizing your dreams is easier if you don't feel you are under a heavy cloud the moment you open your eyes every day. I know this feeling is something we all grapple with, and because many of us do not realize there could be a way to stop feeling like this, we just think we are stuck.

Now tell me, what would your life look like if you were totally set free from mental torment, feeling worthless, and just not feeling good about yourself?

2

Make Up your Mind

What we want to do is move to the next stage toward the transformation you crave. Perhaps you want to recognize those damaging thoughts and stop them from influencing your life? You desire to walk in authority so you are not swayed by daily stress. You are determined to gain control of your mind to find freedom, peace, and clarity. You are looking for strategies so you can become immovable when dealing with life's challenges. You want to take hold of God's promises for your life, and you want to feel confident and carefree. You are determined to take action, to make-over your mind. If you are saying yes, yes, yes, I'm so excited!

The first thing you have to do is decide, because you cannot make-over your mind until you make up your mind that you want to change. When you are tired of living the way you are living, and you are ready to put in the action in order to get the results, nothing good will happen just by wishing. We really have to put energy into action. We have to be active in taking the authority that God says we have, and activate what the Word freely gives us. I am going to give you some insights about how you can do just that, but before I do, I want to give you a little background story.

My story begins in South Africa where I was born. I have lived in three countries, in South Africa, England, and the US. My family and I have been living in Charlotte for almost twelve years now. Living in the southern part of America, some people think I'm from the south because of my accent, but way, way south! All three of my babies were born in different countries, so each of them holds a different passport (you should see the immigration control officers' face when we go through customs every time we travel). I have become accustomed to living in different cultures and in different countries.

Back in my days in South Africa, I was trained as a TV host and a broadcaster, and I have worked in TV production on and off for several years. This is so embarrassing to admit, but I had that bad 90's hairspray hairstyle and wardrobe styling. Those were the days of analog TV, VHS tapes, and film cameras! When we moved to England, I had the opportunity to use my skills as a TV host for a live breakfast morning show "York Today." I had the fabulous opportunity to meet so many people and hear about their stories. I loved interviewing people about where they are, and where their lives were headed. Over the years, I took those skills and in 2013 started my own web TV interview show "Mimika TV" before the days of Facebook Live. As you can probably tell, I love to talk. I love to be able to ask a lot of questions and I love to be able to figure things out and I love to learn. My parents always called me the family chatterbox!

If you follow me on Instagram and Facebook, you'll see a lot of my photos and quotes and memes appear there, because I love to be able to provide positive feedback and positive encouragement. That is just me in a nutshell. Chatty and happy. For 15 years I was a professional photographer, mainly known for photographing babies and children, and I have written two books about the business of photography. Today I am a branding and marketing strategist, and I work with authors, speakers, and entrepreneurs to help them create a marketing strategy to build their business, brand, and platform. As a Christian author and speaker, I am super passionate about equipping and empowering others to walk in God's truth.

Now the real reason I share all of this with you is not to brag, but to give you the honest and raw truth. Even though you may look at my resume and think, "Wow she's got it all together!" Let me tell you an insider secret. Throughout those years of pursuing accolades and achievements, my mindset was a hot mess! I constantly battled with my self-worth. I constantly struggled with feeling rejected, which is something that began in my childhood, and it just seemed to perpetuate throughout my life. This is probably one of the reasons why I became a people pleaser. My decisions were fear based and I avoided any situation where I would be looked down on, be unfavored, or excluded.

Are there any other people pleasers out there willing to admit it? Yeah we are everywhere and it is confession time. Being a perfectionist and people pleaser is exhausting because there is never an end in sight.

For so many years, I thought that it just was the way that I was. I came from a broken childhood, my parents got divorced when I was 10, and I got severely bullied at thirteen-years-old. I always felt alone, I never was in the "cool" crowd, but preferred to stay at home reading books. I would think, "Well, that is just me, I have to learn to accept it. I'm a product of my childhood. I'm just broken." There was a lot of fear, anxiety, and rejection, and it always seemed to be the same story, just on a different day.

Perhaps you might have the same story. To be honest, it is like I got stuck there for years. The thing is, I never really realized I had a problem. For some of us, we go through life just hobbling along with broken tools, we are able to fake being happy, and we accept that is just the way we are. It is like you get used to seeing things through your own off-colored glasses. But until someone hands you a pair of clear 20/20 eyeglasses that put things into sharp focus, you will just continue living the way you are. You will perpetuate cycle after cycle, over and over again, playing that same old broken record. You find yourself repeating the same mistakes, going around and around the mountain, feeling alone, rejected, and helpless.

Irrespective of what people might see on the outside, they judge. Like in my own instance, people looked at me and thought, "She's got it all, this perfect life and perfect family." But let me tell you honey, that simply is not the truth. For three years, I experienced some of the hardest things I have ever had to endure, such as losing my mother-in-law to cancer, dealing with a child contemplating suicide, and picking up the broken pieces of my heart from a failed business. All at the same time.

I had to go through this very difficult situation with one of my children, and let me tell you, as a mother that totally freaked me out! Once I exhausted everything I could do to help my child in my own strength, it caused me to hit the wall. I could no longer live my life wearing a mask of perfection, pretending that everything was okay, when it clearly was not. These experiences were the catalyst in me digging deep and pursuing my own inner healing through God's redemptive grace.

Being a people pleaser is rough, it is a daily grind. Moving past perfection paralysis is something I have to work on constantly. It is something I have to be aware of, knowing that I'm susceptible to these tendencies. I have to watch myself and be really careful of my mindset and self-talk. It definitely is not the trap I want to fall into again.

Now tell me, are you tired of going around that same mountain too? Would you love to be able to move past it? How would it change your life if you were free from those mental bondages and torment? How would you feel if things were different? If every day that you woke up you did not have to deal with constant negativity, would you be happy?

I'm sure you would probably agree that it is definitely something that we *all* deal with. It is like an easy yes, right? When we put on those eyeglasses of clarity and realize this is not how life was meant to be, we finally make progress. We decide. We choose.

When I asked this question to a group I was coaching; Patricia said, "I'd be much more at peace and productive." Suzanne said, "I would be doing something totally different." Terry said "I would feel more peaceful and excited to wake up." Susan said, "No depression, not many bad attitudes, and the feeling of freedom." Robin said, "Peace, and less worry." Christina said "Becoming more productive." Angela said, "Avoiding the procrastination obstacles." And "The whole mental block, or feeling like you are just not good enough, is debilitating." Diane said, "Things are never quite what they seem, people often judge and envy what they do not know." Mike said, "Once I stopped being the people pleaser, I became closer to God. I learned I only needed to please God, and yes; it is freedom." Amen Mike!

Could this be the kind of thinking that is holding *you* back from achieving all your dreams? Perhaps you are not stepping into the fullness of using your gifts and talents that God has designed and made you for, because of the mental bondages you are trapped in? Freedom is something I think we all crave, no matter where you are in the world. Even those who are perhaps non-believers will agree that being free is one of the biggest goals and blessings we can have in our life.

If you are encountering huge stainless steel doors, blockages, and speed bumps; it might be a sign that your mind is stuck. What I want to encourage you with is this; you don't have to feel alone. A lot of us have been in the same situation, many of us have had to go through very stressful and traumatic experiences. I want to share with you some tools to help you to break free. What I have learned from breaking free from my own mental bondage, is that you need to believe that you are a child of God and you are entitled to it. It is your inheritance in Christ to live in freedom, you just need to reach out and grab it.

3

Three Part Being

Yes, just as you can identify a tree by its fruit, so you can identify people by their actions. - Matthew 7:20

Get your pen and your paper ready, we are going to dive into how to get unstuck from "stinking thinking." I must give credit to Joyce Meyer who originally coined this term. It is so accurate because it conjures up a vivid picture of a heap of garbage stewing in our mind. We have a whole lot of hot mess rotting away, and everything mixes up together. We try to figure things out on our own, and those rotten thoughts make everything else stink. That stinking thinking comes out in our words, our behavior, our moods, and emotions; and it affects everyone around us. By getting yourself free, you are not just freeing yourself. You are freeing those who love you and who are around you, because if you live in freedom and you are living in God's promises, you are going to be impacting others too. I know without a shadow of a doubt, that God ordained you for something great. He has a plan for you, but we need to be able to peel off those layers, remove those grave clothes, so you can really walk in freedom.

The first thing I want to talk to you about is the spirit, soul, and body connection. We are made as a three-part being, in God's image. He created us, and knew us before we were even born. Our spirit is saved at Salvation, when we give our life to the Lord, and instantly we are made new, we are instantly saved in our spirit (which is the inner man or woman). We become Christ-like and Christ lives within us. The body is the temple where the Holy Spirit resides. The soul is made up of our mind, our will, and our emotions.

Spirit, Body, and Soul.

This is a tricky part we often get confused about. Our soul (mind, will, emotions) is not instantly made over and saved at salvation, it still needs work. Our spirit is saved, but our soul is what works itself out into our bodies. This is what we need to put through a renewal process.

I could probably guess that you know of someone who is a believer, who loves the Lord, yet they are still living in a stuck life. They are living in bondage and they have old habits and patterns from their old life they find hard to break. It may just be that they haven't got rid of those sticky things that have held them back in the past. This is when we do soul work. Where we start is with our mind because our mind is where we have our thoughts, our reasoning, and our decision-making.

Our will is our desire to do good or bad and mobilize ourselves into action or inaction. I have three kids and when they were toddlers, it was a battle of the wills. As the parent it was my way or the highway, and there would be a fight when they didn't agree. I vividly remember going grocery shopping with my eldest daughter when she was 2 years old. She would throw a very loud hissy fit in the middle of the grocery aisle when I didn't give in to her demands. I'd be like, "Oh my gosh, there goes a waste of a trip." I would haul her back into the car (along with my newborn in the car seat) feeling very embarrassed while I left the cart abandoned.

Often God experiences the same thing with us. He has to battle with our will in order for us to concede and give in to His perfect will. We think we know better and don't want to give in. Then our emotions are swayed by circumstances, our physical environment affects us, our relationships are broken, and our health is a mess. Then our outward starts affecting our inward; which are our emotions. For years, I was ruled by my emotions. If I woke up one day and the kids were having a bad day, I thought, "I'm going to have a bad day today." I would start the day demotivated, feeling negative, and under sufferance before my feet hit the floor. I'd hit the snooze button, hoping it would go away. I'd end up starting the day off badly before it even got started.

The problem is, we carry the baggage of our past and bad habits. Our circumstances are a product of our decisions, and our decisions start in our mind. If your day is a car wreck, backtrack to where you started from in the first place. What were you thinking when you went down this thought path? Sometimes we have these runaway thoughts and they can be like a runaway train, without a train engineer at its helm. It just goes all sorts of places that we don't want it to go. Thoughts are results of years of habitual bad thinking.

If you have thought a certain way for years (maybe it is the way you have always thought since you were a kid), it has become a habit. The issue is that we don't recognize that we have a problem in the first place. If we don't know we have a problem, how can we fix it? The other issue we have is denial. Maybe we know we have a problem, but we don't want to believe it, or even acknowledge that we have a problem, because we know that means we will have to deal with it. Perhaps you are an ostrich, digging your head in the sand hoping it will go away.

Perhaps you are scared of failure or scared of success. It could be both ends of the spectrum; we end up repeating what feels comfortable. Then we have inner turmoil, our bodies show it with headaches, tiredness, and stomach aches. Do I even need to mention the word stress? Stress is a physical manifestation of what is going on in our spirit, mind, and emotions. There is only so much you can hold onto within yourself, pretending everything is okay until your body just screams help! This is exactly what happened to me when my world came crashing down. The stress of having to deal with a failed business, family issues, and grief, I never gave myself time to rest and recuperate until my body yelled STOP. It showed up in my body, complete utter tiredness and exhaustion, and feeling like the sky was falling on a daily basis, I couldn't get myself out of bed. I finally realized I was suffering from depression. Usually I'm not a depressed type of person, I like to be all bubbly and fun, but sometimes life happens. Even though we might not plan it, along the way, we have created these bad habits of false security. We have created these problems that eventually confound themselves, and then eventually become this huge red stop sign that compels you to stop what you are doing and regroup.

The truth is, habits are hard to break without willpower, but the great news is, we don't need WILL power. We need GOD power!

All of us have some bad habits, whether it is self-depreciation and talking badly about others, or bad eating habits; there's a laundry list of things that we all deal with. At the end of the day, everything starts with a source. There is always cause and effect. Being able to recognize that we have a mindset issue is an accomplishment in itself.

There is a critic in your mind and he is a bully. He constantly wants to knock you down and keep you under the current before you have a chance to swim for the shore. Consider how that critic in your mind talks to you, would you talk to someone like that? It sounds something like "Wow, I don't know what you're thinking girl; you are so fat in those pants. Seriously, do you really think anyone is going to look at you dressed like that? Who is going to love you?" "Oh, my gosh! You wouldn't seriously wear that? You are so stupid. Why would anybody even want to do that?" I mean really, hello. I wouldn't talk to my friends like that and I wouldn't talk to my children like that, so why do I talk to myself like that? Why do we allow this level of conversation to continue? We have to recognize who that bully is, and that bully is the enemy.

This enemy is a very well-trained thespian. He mimics your voice and your tone. He has been watching you since the day you were born and he knows your weak points. He knows how to pretend to make it sound like you are going crazy. He knows how to instigate and poke you in those soft spots, in those weak parts that really hurt. He knows how to play that stuck record of harassment and torment going over and over and over again. Eventually, he wears you down and you start to think and believe it as truth because you have heard it so many times. What happens then is you become weak, you accept it, and you stop fighting. Eventually, if he has worn you down so much, you accept that it is part of who you are and your personality. You give in and you accept it. This is NOT what God wants for you! If you know there is an enemy raging against you, you are going to need to fight.

Often, the results are from roots that we might not realize are there, or are willing to admit we have. Two big roots I talk about in my book, *Worrier to Warrior: A Mother's Journey from Fear to Faith* are the roots of fear and rejection. These roots give rise to trees which grow fruit. The fruit of rejection on one side is feeling like you are never good enough, and on the other side is becoming a people pleaser. The root of rejection could have taken hold as far back as when you were an infant.

The original sources of roots can be endless, so we need to pray and ask the Holy Spirit to reveal the causes of the rotten roots so we can dig them out. I pray that the Holy Spirit brings to your mind and your remembrance and starts to speak to you. If you start remembering experiences or conversations, or old memories pop up; that is how the

Holy Spirit works. He very gently will say, "This is something we need to deal with" Once you ask for clarity and pray for God to reveal them to you, He surely will, and the healing will begin. It just takes this first step.

1 Corinthians 2:16 it says, *"For who can know the Lord's thoughts who knows enough to teach him but we understand these things for we have the mind of Christ."* Now this is a great Scripture to constantly remind yourself, and to repeat over. It's something I do in the mornings before my feet hit the floor, is say, "I have the mind of Christ." Whether I say it over a hundred times a day, I am constantly reminding myself that God's Word says, "I have the mind of Christ and you can renew your mind."

4

Identify Theft

Once you were not a people, but now you are the people of God; once you had not received mercy, but now you have received mercy. - 1 Peter 2:10

P art of the journey to freedom is knowing who you are in Christ, as His child. A lot of us suffer from spiritual identity theft. The enemy has taken so long playing that record, wearing you down; you have forgotten who you are. We need to learn to discern and recognize what is from God, yourself, and the enemy. That voice, like I said, knows how to mimic all types of voices and accents, and he knows how to make it sound like you. Recognizing what is from God and yourself and separating them, will really help you do the next thing, which is, take the thought captive. By taking captive the thoughts that derail you, you will be able to stop them before they get onto the runway train. You are not going to let them leave the station because you are ready to recognize them as something that is not of God.

The way you recognize what is from God is you study the original to recognize the fake. Whether you are looking at money or precious art, the way you are able to recognize a fake is by spending time studying the original. This means for you to learn to recognize the voice of God, you need to saturate yourself in God's Word to learn His tone, his cadence, His flow. If you have saturated yourself in watching negative things on TV or listening to the negative talk radio that goes on and on in your head; you have saturated your soul with things that are not good, so of course it is going to come out in your thinking.

You need to start thinking of flipping the script. For a long time, I stopped watching TV or the news to put a stop to the negative flow. I no longer watch the news because it is too depressing and puts me in a bad mood. I know there are important events happening in the world; but I have decided to pray for peace knowing that God has got it covered. There is nothing I can achieve by worrying, because that will do nothing to change things. I need to keep myself saturated by feeding my spirit with what God's Word says about me.

A big tip I love to do, which I would encourage you to do, is to use a journal to write down your thoughts. When you start tracking your thoughts, ideas and promptings you can tell what words are from God and what words are your inner petulant child. By "brain dumping" your thoughts onto paper, you get them out of your head where they can settle and give you peace of mind (because you are no longer stewing over them). This is something I have been doing since I was a child, and it is something I always encourage others to do. Write down the date and any Scriptures you feel led to read, and any thoughts or questions you might have (kind of like a dear diary). This will help you to celebrate your small wins because you easily forget how far you have come, which can cause you to give up prematurely.

Any good coach knows to track progress, whether you are an athletic coach or a business coach, you need to be able to track your progress so you can see how far you have come. There is a well-known concept psychology called "Kaizen" which is *"the Japanese art of relatively small, continuous improvements" (1) or* the power of small wins.

Why is Kaizen so powerful? There are several reasons why the concept of Kaizen is extremely powerful, namely because ; (a) It bypasses the fear response; effectively ending procrastination, (b) the changes become habits and new habits produce permanent results; and (c) small changes, made continually over time, make a huge impact. Each day when you make a conscious decision to put your focus on and find your worth in God, you are creating small wins. Rome was not built in a day, so neither will your mind be made over in a day (no matter the editing tricks we see on TV). We just need to take incremental baby steps, one day at a time.

When we are self-indulgent and so self-focused, we are looking for something that we do not have. It is like trying to withdraw from an ATM where the bank balance is zero. If you have put nothing in the bank, there is going to be zero to take out. What I mean is when you spend time with God focusing on what His Word says about you, you are investing in your spiritual bank balance. When on a day you are feeling low, and you need to make a withdrawal of strength, you will have it.

Do you suffer from self-doubt and feeling worthless? We need to recognize the real source of our value because our value is only found in Jesus Christ when He died and was raised for us. You are a child of God, with an inheritance given freely as a gift, so all you need to do is accept it graciously. Are you a bad gift receiver? I have been guilty of this too, where I am great at giving gifts and compliments, but when someone wants to give me a compliment or a gift I'm like, "No, no, no, I don't need it, no." It is false humility and it causes us to run our bank balance dry. Then we start this ridiculous "Woe is me, I feel low" cycle again, we just need to understand that our acceptance through Christ. It is a gift plain and simple - there is nothing you have to do to earn it. It is yours already, so be a grateful receiver and reach out and take it.

Nothing you can do can make God love you more than He does right now. Isn't that like mind-blowing? In other words, you don't have to do anything, because He loves you already. He knew what He was getting when He saved you and when you were born. He knew what your life was going to look like. You are not a big surprise for Him, He understands you better than you understand yourself. He has created these prizes for us and all we need to do is stand up and take up the prize. As children of God, this is our inheritance. As soon as we were adopted into God's family; we are immediately given a crown, and a robe, and are made royal. It is time to walk in victory because of God's promises. Keep your head up high darling; don't let your crown fall off. Isn't it time that you claim what is rightfully yours?

God says He will never leave you nor forsake you (that is in Deuteronomy 31:8). Salvation is a gift, you don't have to earn it (see Ephesians 2:8). We are dead to sin and alive in Christ (see Romans 6:12). This means that we don't have to let sin reign and rule in our life. Our present sufferings don't compare to our future glory. Even though it might feel like our life is challenging, experiencing suffering is creating endurance; and endurance creates character where we get stronger and stronger. It is like a muscle we build over time, because we will eventually be strong enough to fight the good fight, and receive our glory that God has for us. Are you ready to take back your authority as a child of God and get victory? I'm sure this is a no-brainer question right?

Prayer to restore your Identity in Christ:
Dear Lord Jesus. Thank you for dying on the cross so that I can become a new creation. I accept that my identity is only found in You, and I let go of any preconceived ideas that are not of You. I break off the broken orphan spirit over me in Jesus name, help me to believe that I am your royal child. I pray that you bring me into total alignment with God's will for my life. Amen!

5

Negative Thoughts

We destroy arguments and every lofty opinion raised against the knowledge of God, and take every thought captive to obey Christ. - 2 Corinthians 10:5

R enown South African cognitive neuroscientist, Dr. Caroline Leaf, has spent her life's work studying the brain and the effects of thoughts. She says; "*75% to 95% of the illnesses that plague us today are a direct result of our thought life.* What we think about affects us physically and emotionally. It's an epidemic of toxic emotions." (1) Dr. Leaf goes on to say that "*Research shows that fear, all on its own, triggers more than 1,400 known physical and chemical responses and activates more than 30 different hormones. There are INTELLECTUAL and MEDICAL reasons to FORGIVE! Toxic waste generated by toxic thoughts causes the following illnesses: diabetes, cancer, asthma, skin problems and allergies to name just a few.* "

There have been several breakthrough studies that suggest that we may have far more control over how our brains function (our thoughts, behaviors, and emotions) than we previously assumed. The Big Think says; "By learning how to control our thinking, we may be able to deliberately reshape our neural pathways and rewire our brains to make ourselves more successful and fulfilled. In other words, shape your brain and you can shape your life." (2)

Toxic emotions are a result of toxic thoughts. It is so important that we start each day with good thinking habits to protect our minds and our physical health. Making sure we cover our minds with the armour of God before our feet hit the floor in the morning, is how we start our day right. We do not want to keep ourselves stuck in despair, and prevent our blessings from flowing, so it is imperative that we take each thought captive. We do not want our stinking thinking to become a runaway train, in fact we should not allow the negative train to leave the station!

It is our job to choose to stop the thought as soon as it appears. The Holy Spirit is our helper and will gently remind you when a thought has been sent by the enemy. For example, when we are bombarded with a spirit of fear that brings the feeling of dread, we revoke access by sending the spirit back to the pit. We speak the truth, which is God's Word, so in this case you would say "God has not given me a spirit of fear but of power, love and a sound mind. You spirit of fear be gone in Jesus name!" (2 Timothy 1:7). The spirit will have no choice but to vacate immediately. That is how we take every thought captive to make it obedient to Christ.

When in doubt, repent. Repentance brings us back into alignment with God and revokes any access the enemy might have over your mind, body, and soul. Every word and every action starts with a thought so it is very important to train our thoughts to be God's thoughts.

Isaiah 55:8
For my thoughts are not your thoughts, neither are your ways my ways,"
declares the LORD.
    See also Matthew 9:4, Matthew 15:19, Job 20:2, Isaiah 55:9, Romans 2:15.

Prayer: Release from Negative Thoughts

Dear Lord, I thank you for the redeeming power of Jesus who died and was raised from the dead for me. I repent for dwelling on any negative, evil, wrong thoughts, and bring my mind into obedience to Christ. I seal up any access points that my thoughts have given to the enemy and I seal my mind with the blood of Jesus and wear the helmet of salvation. Thank you for saving me in Jesus name amen!

6

Anxiety

Do not be anxious about anything, but in every situation, by prayer and petition, with thanksgiving, present your requests to God. - Philippians 4:6

C ontrol Freaks Anonymous is recruiting for their team, are you already a member of the club? No do not answer that, it is probably why it is called the "Anonymous" club. Confession time, I've been a member for many years and did not even know it. Now anxiety is no joking matter, it is a debilitating state of being that affects millions of people every day. According to the Anxiety and Depression Association of America, (1) "Anxiety disorders are the most common mental illness in the U.S., affecting 40 million adults in the United States age 18 and older, or 18.1% of the population every year. Anxiety disorders are highly treatable, yet only 36.9% of those suffering receive treatment."

Physical symptoms display themselves as stomach aches, lump in the throat, the fight or flight reaction, sweaty hands, irritability, attention deficit, the list goes on. Living in a constant state of fight or flight, taxes our adrenal system and is not good for the body. A visit to a doctor made this abundantly clear when she said the stress from the anxiety I had been under was causing my body severe adverse effects. If I did not chill and learn to live at a normal rhythm, I could have long-term ill effects. Anxiety is closely related to fear and worry (they all hang out together at the lunch table). The spirits of torment that are rooted in fear show themselves as anxiety and worry. They steal your peace and want to kill and destroy your joy.

The Office of the Surgeon General (2) conducted a study of combat soldiers who served in Iraq. The findings concluded that the level of combat was the main determinant of a soldier's mental health status. The length of deployment and family separations were considered the top mitigating factor, as does multiple deployments that showed higher acute stress and was related to higher rates of mental health problems and marital conflict. The suicide rates amongst combat soldiers were higher than the average army rate. PTSD is considered common place amongst those experiencing high levels of conflict, combat, and threats to one's life.

In today's society our levels of stress are off the charts. Many individuals are displaying the same signs of stress that a soldier with PTSD who has been exposed to multiple stressors. The findings of a study (3) that appeared in the December issue of the American Psychological Association's (APA) Journal of Personality and Social Psychology said the average high school student today has the same level of anxiety as the average psychiatric patient had in the early 1950's! This is shocking.

The temporary emotion of anxiety is experienced as a reaction to a particular situation or perceived threat. With all the mod cons we have access to today, we are suffering more than ever before. Excess causes anxiety. We are loaded with lists. Our clutter crushes our calm. We might be connected to thousands of "friends" on Facebook, yet we are the most disconnected generation. We are creating less meaningful relationships and connections that the isolation is crushing our mental state of well-being. The perceived threats we are exposed to due to information overload have contributed to this mental epidemic.

The Merriam-Webster dictionary defines the word anxious as "characterized by extreme uneasiness of mind or brooding fear about some contingency, ardently or earnestly wishing, characterized by, resulting from, or causing anxiety, worrying." Are you a brooder? Brooding is described as, "moodily or sullenly thoughtful or serious, darkly somber." Wow we are a bucket full of sunshine!

According to the World happiness report of 2017 (4) happiness is both social and personal. There are six variables that were measured to determine the index, and half were due to differences in having someone to count on, generosity, a sense of freedom, and freedom from corruption. In richer countries, the differences were not explained only by income inequality, but by the differences in mental health, physical health, and personal relationships. The study found that the largest single source of misery is mental illness. In 2007, the USA ranked third among the OECD happiest countries where in 2016, it had dropped to the nineteenth. In all three Western countries, diagnosed mental illness emerges as more important than income, employment, or physical illness. You would think that eliminating poverty, unemployment and physical illness would be a huge factor; however, these three factors barely make as much difference as mental illness on its own. The other eye-opening finding is that in the USA, for example, a person who is poor is 5.5 percentage points more likely than otherwise to be miserable. By contrast, someone with depression or anxiety is 10.7 percentage points more likely to be miserable. It costs money to reduce misery, but the cheapest of the policies is treating depression and anxiety disorders. Imagine if we could miraculously abolish depression and anxiety disorders without changing anything else?

An important factor they uncovered is that many of the problems of adulthood can be traced back to childhood and adolescence. The strongest predictor of a satisfying adult life is not qualifications but a combination of the child's emotional health and behaviour. The survey in the World Happiness report consisted of data compiled from a very detailed survey of all children born in the English County of Avon in 1991/2 who have been followed intensively up until today. The study compared family income, parenting style, parental engagement, and involvement, and conflict between parents. They discovered that the worst factor of all for children's emotional health and behaviour is a mother who is mentally ill, more so than the father's mental state. This means that us mothers have the most important influence on the future well-being of our children, so we owe it to ourselves and to our children to be healthy, mentally.

Feeling anxious comes down to an issue of control. If we cannot control the outcome, we get our knickers in a twist and freak out. If you notice the dictionary mentions "wishing." Anxiety is based on us worrying about some possible outcome that may or may not happen, wishing for the best. Last time I checked nobody got anything by "wishing."

God's Word is bursting with Scriptures that says, "Don't be anxious" with 365 mentions in the Bible; Philippians 4:6, Psalm 139:23, Ecclesiastes 2:22, Matthew 6:34, Luke 10:41, Luke 12:26, Matthew 6:31 to name a few.

If we do not deal with the root causes, the tree of anxiety will keep on blooming. Let's be honest, the root cause of our anxiety is based in a deep seated distrust. What we are really saying when we are anxious is that we do not trust God to work things out for our good. We are not confident that He knows the best outcome for our lives and will do what He says He will do, so we prefer to brood about things and remain anxious. Perhaps it is a habit from your past and you do not know how else to live without feeling anxious about everything. The world (which is influenced by the devil) wants us to believe that anxiety is something we just have to live with. Many conditions are labeled as disorders when what they truly are is a demonic assault on our bodies, minds, and souls to get us weak and wounded. We need to stop agreeing with the devil by accepting labels, conditions, and disorders as normal; and start putting up a fight so we can get set free.

If we prefer to live our lives filled with fear and anxiety, then God cannot deliver us. We need to choose to let go and let God be the creator that we know Him to be, and let Him work things out. If you do not fully trust God then you need to dig deeper and ask why. As born again believers, if we believe that the Bible is God's truth, then why do we take pieces, but leave other pieces out? If God said, "Stop worrying, I've got this," then we need to hand in our badge and retire our membership from the Control Freaks Anonymous Club. Being set free from anxiety starts with developing an attitude of gratitude, we cannot be grateful and grumpy at the same time. Focusing on our blessings and the good things in life, helps us to reframe our thinking. What we focus on grows, so feed your faith not your fears!

Prayer: Release from Anxiety

Thank you, Lord for Your unfailing love. I choose to place my trust in You. Please deliver me from anxiety and break off the spirit of fear. With Your strength I take captive every negative thought that tries to steal my joy. I thank you Lord for delivering me from the spirit of fear and anxiety. In Jesus' name, amen!

Please note: Always follow the advice of your medical practitioner when it comes to treating issues of anxiety and mental health.

7

Worry

Therefore I tell you, do not worry about your life, what you will eat or drink; or about your body, what you will wear, is not life more than food and the body more than clothes? Look at the birds of the air: They do not sow or reap or gather into barns—and yet your Heavenly Father feeds them. Are you not much more valuable than they? - Matthew 6: 25-26

Van Wilder said "Worrying is like a rocking chair, it gives you something to do, but doesn't get you anywhere." Joyce Meyer says "Worry is a down payment on a problem you may never have." I love this analogy because it is so true. When we worry we might think we are putting our energy to good use because there is lots of swaying back and forth, but at the end of the day we are still stuck in the exact same spot as when we started.

Worry is a gang member of that fear party, always trying to take us out using its fear tactics. For some of us it feels like worry has become part of our personality; "I'm a worry wart, I always worry about things, it is a family thing worrying all the time." Let me tell you, sugar, that is agreeing with the devil! Who in their right mind would want to willingly agree with the lie that worry is an effective use of energy? Saying words of worry and agreeing with the negative will only keep you stuck in that defeated cycle.

Matthew 6:27
  Can all your worries add a single moment to your life?

The definition of 'worry' according to the Merriam-Webster dictionary **(1)** is "to harass by tearing, biting, or snapping especially at the throat, to shake or pull at with the teeth a terrier worrying a rat, to touch or disturb something repeatedly, to change the position of or adjust by repeated pushing or hauling, to assail with rough or aggressive attack or treatment, to subject to persistent or nagging attention or effort, to afflict with mental distress or agitation, to make anxious, to torment."

Did you get that? Harassing, tearing, biting, snapping, shaking, pulling, disturbing, pushing, hauling, assail, rough, aggressive, attack, nagging, afflict, distress, agitation, torment. This sounds like a violent attack that can only result in the victim being destroyed, abused, and even killed! Last time I checked the Bible there was zero, nil, zilch, nada times it mentions any of this as acceptable for God's children. In fact it says the exact opposite, so why would we willingly agree to this kind of treatment if we know that the only outcome is destruction? Get a grip girl!

Worry shows us that we do not trust God. Wow for God that is got to hurt! We know we are His child, yet we push away His hand of help because we do not trust Him enough to take care of our situation. Worrying about the future and things we cannot control robs us of today's blessings. Our bodies reflect our inner turmoil and worry exhibits itself in physical symptoms like headaches, stomach aches, loss of appetite, loss of sleep etc.

Proverbs 12:25

Worry weighs a person down; an encouraging word cheers a person up.

The truth of the matter is that no amount of worrying adds a single moment to our lives, but takes away moments of joy, peace, faith, and love. The opposite of worry is trust, peace, joy, patience, contentment, being even tempered, and generally much more pleasant to get along with. Wouldn't you want that for your life? If you have decided enough is enough, you need to take an active role in casting out those punks of fear and worry.

Jesus said in Luke 12:4-7

4 "I tell you, my friends, do not be afraid of those who kill the body and after that can do no more. 5 But I will show you whom you should fear: Fear him who, after your body has been killed, has authority to throw you into hell. Yes, I tell you, fear him. 6 Are not five sparrows sold for two pennies? Yet not one of them is forgotten by God. 7 Indeed, the very hairs of your head are all numbered. Don't be afraid; you are worth more than many sparrows.

More references can be found in Luke 12:22-24, Matthew 6:25, Luke 21:14, and my favorite is;

2 Timothy 1:7

For God has not given us a spirit of fear, but of power and of love and of a sound mind.

As soon as you start feeling worried, recognize it as a spirit out to torment you, and use your mouth to speak God's truth from His Word. Speak 2 Timothy 1:7 Scripture out loud to help you get the victory and start creating good thinking habits by taking every thought captive into the obedience of Christ.

Prayer: Release from Worry

Thank you Lord that Your Word says that you don't give me a spirit of fear but divine power, love and a sound mind through Jesus. I thank you Lord that I can put my trust in You to work all things out for my good. I cast out the spirit of fear and worry and command it to go now in Jesus' name. I plead the blood of Jesus over my mind and heart and protect myself with the armor of God so that I can fight off the attacks of the enemy. Thank you for delivering me in Jesus' name. Amen!

8

The Mind is the Battlefield

For we wrestle not against flesh and blood, but against principalities, against powers, against the rulers of the darkness
of this world, against spiritual wickedness in high places. –
Ephesians 6:12

H ave you had one of those days that seem to go from bad to
worse? Like it never rains but pours? Oftentimes, it is a result
of our own bad attitude and choices, and sometimes it is no
fault of our own. But sometimes, it is the enemy who is trying to steal
your joy and peace.

The place the enemy likes to attack us first is our minds, then he goes for
our emotions. If he can get us to question our purpose, our calling, our
destiny; he can stop us from walking out the plan God has for our lives
and our loved ones. As soon as we recognize the minefield trap that is
our cranky teenager, that petulant child, or the kids who keep fighting;
we can learn to detect an attack of division and discord immediately
and prevent it from derailing our day and our destiny.

If we can stop the enemy from winning the battle in our minds, we can stop him in his tracks from winning the war. The smartest thing we can do is recognize the attack, focus on God, and not give up. God has said we are already conquerors, so do not concede defeat simply because you do not think you can win. If you really believed that you could not lose, wouldn't you go in the fight confidently knowing that the God of all the universe has already given you the victory?

Romans 8:37...

No, in all these things we are more than conquerors through him who loved us.

Then it is about time we take up our prize, step up, and claim what is rightfully ours. The first step is to take captive those thoughts of insurrection that are trying to derail your progress by learning to recognize what is of God, your own thoughts and the enemy. Just imagine the battle cry you would give out when you are confident that the weapons you have at your disposal are already primed in your favor to win!

Learning to discern will become one of the strongest tools in your arsenal and the only way to sharpen the blade of truth is to know the truth. Once you know the original, you will recognize the fake, the fraud, the phony. It is important to dismiss those ramblings that are designed to take you down by stealth as soon as they pop into your head to make you question yourself. If you do not know the strategy, you are already defeated. Once you know the strategy, you can aim your darts at the bull's eye and take down the enemy's weapons with precision.

Prayer for Protection over your Mind:

Dear Lord Jesus thank you for your sacrifice so that I may live a life of freedom. I break of all mental bondages and blockages hindering my walk in Jesus name. I decree and declare that I am free! I plead the blood of Jesus over my mind and and only allow God's thoughts to fill my mind, heart and soul. Amen!

9

Strongholds & Doors

No, in all these things we are more than conquerors through him who loved us. - Romans 8:37

I love the Scripture Romans 8:37. When we break it down, we realize that we are *more* than conquerors. A conqueror always makes me think of Alexander the Great, conquering the world and taking over territories, and enjoying the spoils of war. God allows us to do the same through Jesus' atonement of sin. By what Jesus did for us, we are able to charge forth with our armor, sword of the spirit, and a shield of faith, and blast through the enemy's camp.

Isn't it about time that we take back what is rightfully ours? Just like the story of David and the Battle of Ziklag where he and his army of men went out to fight. They came back to their camp and discovered that the enemy had plundered the campsite, taken away their kids, their wives, and all their belongings. What happened next, was that all of David's men started blaming *him*! "It is all your fault, look what you did. Now if we had never been away, we would have been able to save or stop them." It was insurrection. So what did David do? He didn't get into a heated argument and tell the guys off. He didn't blast at them and start blaming them either. What did he do? He stayed in praise. He was thankful for what God was going to do because God had already given him his promise; he knew he was going to win. David prayed about it and he trusted that God would bring him success, because as a conqueror he knew he had already won. That is the whole difference. No matter what the circumstances looked like, David relied on what God said and believed that he was already a conqueror.

Jesus died so we can have the authority to live in abundance, health, and happiness. There are so many Scriptures in the Bible that attest to this. If you go to search on one of my favorite tools biblehub.com, you can put in a word and it will bring up a list of Scriptures containing that word. If you search the word 'abundance,' you will see a plethora of Scriptures that relate to that. Health and happiness are your promises. Sometimes you might need to do this to remind yourself, and write it down so you don't forget that it is your inheritance. "I'm a conqueror!" means I have already won the war and I have the rights to spoils of war.

How do we activate the power of God's Word and walk in victory? Often times, the enemy steals our inheritance through open doors that we have allowed him through. You are a Child of God and you have this inheritance, but sometimes it feels like there is this brick wall, stainless steel door, or glass ceiling that is holding you back from receiving the fullness of the gift of salvation. You know it is within touching distance, you can taste it. Perhaps you see others receiving their blessings that are walking in breakthrough, yet your breakthrough seems so far away? Maybe you ask "What is wrong with me, God? Why do I have to go through this? When will this ever end?" Perhaps you have been praying fervently, yet something is pressing replay on the same things over and over, and you have become so frustrated because you are stuck.

Some words I feel I need to share about the concept of the enemy. Now, we cannot abscond our responsibility and blame the devil for every woe we experience. I am not advising you look for a demon behind every door knob, but being aware that there is a spiritual world that we can cannot see, is half the battle. Many charismatic Christians have been taught for years to point to the enemy and say "the devil made me do it". No my friends, we have a choice. Yes, the devil can tempt you, test you, and try you; but inevitably it is up to you to make the choice or not to take the bait. However, you do need to know that there is another realm that influences our realm, and believing what God says about it is so important. By simply placing our hands over our eyes and denying the devil's existence will not help either. There is a battle raging and it is about time we take responsibility for our actions, step up, take action and fight!

Let me tell you this, the devil is a legalist. He knows his rights and he is going to exercise his rights. Just like in the book of Job where the enemy was in front of the Lord, accusing Job saying, "Look at Job. The only reason he loves you is because he has all those worldly possessions, the blessing and the wealth that you have given him." Then God said, "Well you can test him, but don't kill him." Sometimes I wonder, that was a little unfair. Why was the enemy allowed to be in the courts in front of God in the first place? I was so confused about the situation.

Digging deeper, I realized that everything in Heaven works under a protocol. There is a system of doing things and a legal system the heavens and earth abide by. When we talk about the courts of Heaven, we need to remember that God is the ultimate judge who sits on the throne and judges. What you need to know is, the devil knows what his rights are, and given any chance, he will accuse *you* because he is called the "accuser of the brethren." You are the defendant in the courts of Heaven, he is the prosecutor and he is going to find any tiny little bit of evidence to use against you to bring cause to interfere in your life. He might say, "Look, she is praying for a breakthrough, but look what she did here, and look what she said there."

This is why we should be grateful we have Jesus because He is our lawyer and our advocate. We only need to remember that sometimes things are hidden, and we don't know what they are. Often, these invisible barriers to success can be due to open doors that we need to shut. We fight in the spiritual realm. In Scripture it talks about strongholds that keep us in bondage, and strongholds are things that we often can't see. 2 Corinthians 10:4 is says "The weapons we fight with are not the weapons of the world. On the contrary, they have divine power to demolish strongholds."

Let me go through a couple of strongholds, and open doors, and see what triggers your memory. Make some notes if you feel like the Holy Spirit is talking to you about this. A lot of times, our strongholds are roots of fear from perhaps trauma, past hurt, or abuse, and it could be something that happened to you when you were very young. Perhaps you went through a traumatic event; you lost a family member, were in a car accident, experienced divorce (as the child or adult), or experienced any kind of physical, mental, or emotional trauma. Any kind of trauma can create an open door. Trauma creates an opening in our heart that allows things like fear, anxiety, worry to attach to us. Once we are hurt or we become wounded, we become incredibly sensitive. When our feelings are hurt again we can physically feel it. It's like being a human pin cushion or it's like a soccer punch to the gut.

Another huge root is rejection, whether it is from abandonment or feeling unloved, or not feeling accepted. My personal experience was being the child of divorce and being bullied at school, and that followed me around for years. My mind would constantly play that broken record about how I was never good enough, no one wanted to be my friend, and it affected me right into adulthood. Whether a parent abandoned you, or perhaps you were divorced or bullied, it could have been something recent or something ancient. Rejection is a very deep-seated invisible root that we don't often see, but it displays itself in other ways.

Now here is a biggie, unforgiveness. God's Word says that He will not forgive you if you do not forgive others. In the Lord's Prayer, it says, "forgive us our trespasses as we forgive those who trespass against us." I believe that the reason why that line is there is because of the protocol of Heaven. In the courts of Heaven, in order for God to forgive you, you need to forgive others first. If you have any unforgiveness toward anyone, it is a legal door opener that Satan is going to exploit to accuse you. How can God give you what you will not give others?

Another door opener is bitterness that eventually turns to anger and hatred. Those feelings can be deep-seated, and if you trace them back, they usually are roots of fear and rejection. Perhaps you become bitter and angry from how you were once treated, and instead of allowing yourself to feel rejected again, you have built up a wall of bitterness.

Another big door opener that people do not consider or dismiss is occult activities. Even if you were a child, innocently playing with something like the Ouija board, or seeing a fortune-teller, or believing in horoscopes, or anything that is occult in nature is a door opener. Sometimes we do it very innocently; not thinking that these actions are planting roots. It is all about legality. We have allowed the enemy into our lives (either knowingly or unknowingly) and said okay we agree with the darkness and opened our minds and our hearts to the dark side. Personally, I don't watch scary movies because I know they mess with my peace of mind. This is something that I am very careful about; I always protect myself by pleading the blood of Jesus over my mind when I'm exposed to something suspect. Now don't get your knickers in a twist; it is not about seeing a devil under every tree. What I am talking about is protecting my gates, which are my eyes and my ears. I want to filter what I am allowing in and really make sure to keep those doors closed. Once you have opened a door, you have to go through a process of repentance. It is not hard, but it is something you will have to be conscious of. Being vigilant is important so that you don't leave those doors a little ajar; let us make sure we shut them.

Another big door opener is generational curses. Perhaps you might think, "I've never heard of curses, which are just something you see in the movies." No, in actual fact, part of Jesus' ministry was healing the sick, raising the dead, expelling demons, and breaking curses. What we need to understand is that curses can go back three or four generations. We might not know who our Granddaddy was way back then, but he/she might have been involved in occult activities that opened a door to our family line. Think of the Kennedy family line, isn't it strange that generation after generation has been plagued by premature deaths? Have you considered that perhaps what you are suffering from might not be something due to your own behavior or decisions? Perhaps it is due to a curse that was caused by generational sin? If we open the door to sin by doing things that God tells us not to do; they will remain open and become easy access for us to be attacked, unless we repent and close those doors.

Ephesians 6:12 says, "For we wrestle not against flesh and blood but against principalities, against powers, against the rulers of the darkness of this world, against spiritual wickedness in high places." Again, this is a spiritual war in the spiritual world, not some vain imagination in our mind. We need to know where we stand if we are to break free from the grip of curses.

Prayer for release from Strongholds:

Dear God thank you for your love, grace and protection over my life. I break off all strongholds over my mind, my heart, my body and my soul in Jesus name. I break off any generational strongholds over my family line in Jesus name. I decree and declare that as from today the enemy no longer has a hold on me. I proclaim my inheritance in Christ as a royal child of God and step into my life of freedom. In Jesus name amen!

10

Hope & Healing

But for you who fear my name, the Sun of Righteousness will rise with healing in his wings. And you will go free, leaping with joy like calves let out to pasture. - Malachi 4:2 (NLT)

God wants you completely healed. Often we do not get the help we need because we are shamed into silence. Diane said, "For a very long time, I held on to the trauma of being sexually assaulted and I suffered from PTSD and blamed myself for what happened to me. Only in recent years have I found the strength to even talk about it." I have to applaud Diane for stepping out and being willing to speak about it; because that is the first thing we need to do -be willing to talk about it. Most importantly is that she is reaching out to people who can actually help her.

It is the silence that keeps us from breaking free. Teresa said, "Sometimes I don't think we even realize what happened in our past. Events influence our view of ourselves." Our thinking has becomes so habitual. We forget that it might have started way back then, and we don't recognize its damaging effects today, we have become blind. This is why I say journaling is so important while you are reading the Word.

God will be there speaking to you, and the Holy Spirit will put the pieces together. You may remember something from when you were a kid, and that will help shine a light on it to show you what you need to deal with. You can only deal with a problem and get healing once you recognize it, and put it at Jesus' feet so He can do the divine healing within you.

How do we activate God's Word? I can't say it enough, but forgive, forgive, forgive. Forgiveness is the key to everything. When you don't feel like forgiving, just do it and forgive. Your feelings will eventually catch up to your decisions. It doesn't have to be complicated, just a simple "I'm Sorry Lord, forgive me," will do. That's all it needs to be. You have activated the protocol of heaven. No matter whether you got angry with someone, you lost your temper in traffic, or you had a bad thought; any kind of sin can be easily forgiven. The Holy Spirit does an excellent job of highlighting issues within you, and stirs in you things you should deal with. He is a gentleman, and will never push you, He lovingly urges you to strive for righteousness. None of us are perfect and we all sin, so there is no shame in saying sorry. Don't let pride stop you from fessing up either, just let it go! It is really that simple. As soon as we ask God for forgiveness, He forgives us; and we are sealed by His blood and His protection. Then this allows the legal protocol of Heaven to take over where God closes the doors and seals the access shut. Satan can no longer accuse you and keep you under his control because you have released that sticky thing of what has been holding you back.

We also need to ditch the wilderness, "Woe is me" victim mentality. If you are constantly feeling sorry for yourself having a pity party, saying to yourself, "It's never going to change, it always happens to me." That kind of stinking thinking and speaking is not going to help you get out of your ditch. You really need to stop that and realize that is not getting you anywhere. We need to use the weapons of warfare that God gives us, and one of the biggest weapons is putting on the armor of God. Would you go out for the day half-dressed? You would not put on your shirt and leave off your pants would you? Think about this, as much as you dress your physical body, you need to dress your spiritual body and put on the armor of God which is vitally, vitally important. After being harassed for years by negative thoughts within the first minute of waking, I have developed a new habit and forced myself into praying the armor of God over myself before my eyes are open. As soon as I hit the off button on my alarm in the morning, I immediately pray the armor. Over the years, I created a little song that I taught all my children, and we sing it on the way to school every morning. My youngest daughter knows it very well, it goes: "Thank you for the helmet of salvation, the breastplate of righteousness, the belt of truth, shield of faith, sword of the Spirit and the readiness the gospel of peace on our feet in Jesus' name. Amen!" That is all of it; you are literally clothing yourself from the tip of your head to the tips of your toes with God's armor. Once you are protected, then your feelings won't get hurt when you have that breastplate over your chest. Your mind will not be wandering on all sorts of things because the helmet of salvation protects it. You can take an active role and speak God's truth to cut through those negative thoughts. I cannot emphasize enough how important it is to do this on a daily basis.

The other big thing is to fully submit to God in obedience because really, obedience is better than sacrifice. Honest truth, this is one of the things I battle with the most, is aligning my will to God's will. I am the one who says, "Don't worry God, I got this. I am praying for that thing, but I got this. I know how to do this, just let me do it." I am a fixer; anyone who knows me knows that if there is a problem, I am going to find the best way to fix it. It is part of the way my brain works as a strategist. I am always looking for solutions. Oftentimes I have gotten so used to relying on my own strengths, that I think I don't need God. However, He showed me very clearly that I couldn't rely on me when everything fell apart and I came to the end of my rope. Once I had exhausted myself and I was physically depressed and exhausted, I had reached the bottom of the barrel. Only then did I concede defeat and take up His light and easy yoke. Stupid of me, I know!

I have to obey God because God knows better than me. He can see the obstacles before they come my way. If God has been speaking to you about being obedient, why are you resisting? If you are confused about what to do, go back to the last thing He told you to do, because obedience is systematic. Unless you have finished the last thing He told you, He will not give you the second or the third step. So go back to what He told you to do last and do that first.

The other tip is to see things with new eyeglasses. Finding clarity is about keeping your mind saturated in the Word. By taking every thought captive, as that thought comes in your mind you stop it in its tracks, "That was a really stupid thing for you to do. I can't believe you, you are..." STOP! Sorry that is not going to work, pause, delete, and purge. Decide that you are not going to allow that to continue. You have to confess with your mouth that "I have the mind of Christ" daily even if you say it a million times. Even if you don't feel like it, just confess it because there is power in your words. There is power of life and death in what you say. One thing I want to add is to really watch and censor your words because negative words are part of the problem, too. If you keep confessing with your mouth that you are not good enough, you are agreeing with the enemy and you are not moving yourself forward. Make sure that you censor your words carefully.

One thing that I have done that has helped me tremendously is to print and recite God's Word so I can say it out loud. You will rewire your thinking because as it says in the Scripture, faith comes by the Word of God and only by hearing it. This means that when you speak something out loud and you hear it, you start to rewire your brain and create new ways of thinking. Even though you might have thought some old way for years, when you start speaking positive out loud, it will start to rewire the way that you think. This is definitely something that will give you confidence that you *can* change the way you think.

Finding a friend for support and encouragement is important because we all need a coach. It is like trying to go on a diet solo. It is really hard to stay motivated if you don't have someone keeping you accountable. This is why Weight Watchers is so popular; it has built in accountability and support when members regularly attend meetings. People will ask, "How are you doing this week?" and keep you on track.

Matthew 18:18-19 says, "*Assuredly, I say to you whatever you bind on earth will be bound in heaven and whatever you loose on earth will be loosed in heaven. Again I say unto you that if two of you agree on earth concerning anything they ask, it will be done for them by My Father in heaven.*"

Aren't those awesome words that Jesus spoke? All we need to do is stand together, pray together and activate the promises of God. Obviously God will not just give us everything we want, but He certainly will give us everything we need because He is a good, good Father. You have the rights to your inheritance and the power through Jesus' name to claim the promises God has for you, so decide to make up your mind and make-over your life!

Extra Offers

Complimentary Study Guide

Download the accompanying study guide by going to:
www.mimikacooney.com/mindset

More Resources

For a list of all my books and other resources visit my website:
https://www.mimikacooney.com

Review

Your opinions are important and I truly value your feedback. As an author it is so important to get **reviews** so that future readers can make better decisions. Please help me by leaving your honest review on your preferred bookstore or platform. Thank you!

Free Store Discount

Would you like graphics, printable prayers, eBooks, wall art, screen-savers, stock images, T-shirts and Merchandise? Use this coupon to get **$5 FREE** to spend in my shop at:
https://www.shopmimika.com

COUPON CODE: **MMOBOOKOFFER**

References

Scriptures reference the New International Version bible unless otherwise noted.

Chapter 1 - Are you Stuck?

Chapter 2 - Make Up your Mind

Chapter 3 - Three Part Being

Chapter 4 - Identity Theft

1. Kaizen: http://bit.ly/2Mf6uI6 (July 17, 2018).

Chapter 5 - Negative Thoughts

1. Dr. Caroline Leaf: https://drleaf.com/about/toxic-thoughts/
2. Rewire brain: https://bigthink.com/experts-corner/how-to-rewire-your-brain-for-success

Chapter 6 - Anxiety

(1) Anxiety: Anxiety and Depression Association of America "Anxiety disorders" https://adaa.org/about-adaa/press-room/facts-statistics# (3/29/2018).

(2) Anxiety: The Office of the Surgeon General study of combat soldiers http://i.a.cnn.net/cnn/2007/images/05/04/mhat.iv.report.pdf (3/29/2018).

(3) Anxiety: American Psychological Association's (APA) Journal of Personality and Social Psychology http://www.apa.org/news/press/releases/2000/12/anxiety.aspx (3/29/2018).

(4) Anxiety: World Happiness report 2017 http://worldhappiness.report/ed/2017/ (3/31/2018).

Chapter 7 - Worry

(1) Worry: Merriam-Webster dictionary "worry" https://www.merriam-webster.com/dictionary/worry (3/31/2018).

Chapter 8 - The Mind is the Battlefield

Chapter 9 - Strongholds & Doors

Chapter 10 - Hope & Healing

Made in the USA
Coppell, TX
14 November 2019

11347177R00031